# LITTLE LIBRARY

# Jungle Animals

Christopher Maynard

# Kingfisher Books

NEW YORK

# Contents

# Jungle life

M ore kinds of animals and plants live and grow in jungles than in all the rest of the world.

Some scientists think there may be over two million kinds of plants and animals there altogether. But because no one has been able to find or count them all yet, we aren't sure just how many there are.

# Where are they?

The biggest jungles are in the tropics which are on either side of the equator. This is the imaginary line that circles the middle of the Earth. On the map below, the tropical jungle areas are marked in green.

In the tropics, the climate is warm and damp, which makes jungles a good home for lots of insects as well as for plants and other animals. Jungles are also known as rain forests, because it rains there nearly every day.

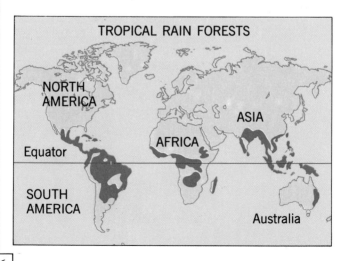

TROPICAL RAIN FORESTS

NORTH AMERICA

ASIA

AFRICA

Equator

SOUTH AMERICA

Australia

# THE SOUTH AMERICAN RAIN FOREST

The biggest rain forest is in South America. It stretches for a long way on both sides of the Amazon River.

Apart from all the trees, creepers, and shrubs, the forest is also full of all kinds of animals. Deadly snakes hang from the branches, while jaguars hunt among the bushes. Brightly-colored frogs live in the pools. Monkeys chatter in the trees above and butterflies flutter through the air looking for food.

# Living in layers

P lant life in the jungle grows in four layers like a great green sandwich. The richest layer is in the high, leafy canopy where there is always a good supply of food. This is where most of the jungle creatures live and feed.

### 1 The top layer
The tallest trees in the jungle grow as high as 180 feet (55 m). They push through the thick layer underneath to get extra sunlight.

### 2 The canopy layer
Here the trees are about 100 feet (30 m) tall. All their leaves grow at the top of the trunk, so little sunlight gets to the ground below.

### 3 The middle layer
These thin, spindly trees form a layer about 50 feet (15 m) high. They grow where light finds a way through the thick canopy above.

### 4 The shrub layer
Plants need light to grow, so the gloomy forest floor has only a few kinds of shrubs, ferns, and fungi among the dead leaves and branches.

# A mini-jungle

I n the jungle, all the rain and hot sun make it very warm and damp underneath the leafy canopy. Plants can grow there all year round.

Try making a mini-jungle of your own at home.

①

**1** You will need a seed tray with holes, some earth and sand, a tray, a spoon, a watering can, a plastic fish tank, and small potted plants like ferns, African violets and begonias.

**2** Fill the seed tray with earth. Put some sand in the big tray. Dampen the smoothed sand. Put the seed tray in the middle of the sand.

②

The secret is to keep your plants warm and give them moist air and soil. A plastic fish tank makes a perfect place for your mini-jungle. The tank will protect the plants from drafts and keep the moist air in. Your plants will grow more quickly than if they were kept in pots on a windowsill.

③

**3** Dig a hole in the earth. Turn a potted plant upside down. Tap the pot base to loosen the plant. Pull out the plant with its soil and place it in the hole. Put in the other plants.

**4** Place the fish tank over the seed tray. Put your jungle in a light place but not in strong sunlight. Always keep the sand damp. In a few months you should have a thriving mini-jungle.

④

# Jungle birds

**M**ore kinds of birds live in jungles than anywhere else in the world. Most of them stay in the canopy where they feed on flowers, fruits, and nuts. A few are hunters. They soar high overhead and swoop down to snatch up bats, other birds, and even monkeys.

IN THE CANOPY

1. Scarlet macaw
2. Greater bird of paradise
3. Hummingbird
4. Toucan
5. African gray parrot
6. Black cockatoo

# Big cats

The most dangerous hunters in the jungle are the big cats. They have the speed and strength to kill almost any other animal.

All the big cats have patterns of spots or stripes on their coats which make them hard to see in the patchy sunlight of the forest floor.

△ Leopards live in Africa and southern Asia. They usually drag their kill up a tree so other animals can't steal it. Leopards often lie along a branch when they snooze.

△ Jaguars live in the tropical forests of Central and South America. They can climb trees, and swim, and often eat fish.

◁ Bengal tigers live in the jungles of India and nearby countries. They hunt alone by hiding in bushes and long grass, and slowly and carefully stalk their prey.

▷ When the tiger is out hunting, it creeps as close as it can to its chosen victim. Then the tiger crouches down and waits for the right moment to make its attack.

◁ In a blur of speed the tiger bursts from its cover, bringing down its startled prey before it even has a chance to get away. The victim is dead within seconds.

15

# In the trees

A pes and monkeys are very good tree climbers, and leap from branch to branch with ease.

Most monkeys use their tails to help them grip the branches and to balance. Apes don't have tails, but three types of ape — chimpanzees (see page 5), gibbons, and orangutans — also live in the trees. They use their hands and feet to grip the branches.

Colobus monkey

Black spider monkey

Entellus langur monkey

Gibbon
(ape)

Orangutan
(ape)

## THE GORILLA

Gorillas are peaceful apes. They spend most of the day hunting for fruit, roots, bark, and leaves to eat. Gorillas spend a lot of time on the ground, but at night they climb into low branches and sleep on beds of twigs.

# Water creatures

Jungles are among the wettest places in the world. Rain collects in huge swamps and lakes, or runs into rivers that flow down to the sea. Wherever there is water, there are all kinds of creatures from tiny insects to large animals like the caiman — a relative of the crocodile.

The Amazon River and the streams that run into it are home to about 2,000 different kinds of fish. Many of them can be seen in tropical fish tanks.

River creatures from the rain forest of South America include huge snakes, fish, eels that give electric shocks, and a giant guinea pig called a capybara.

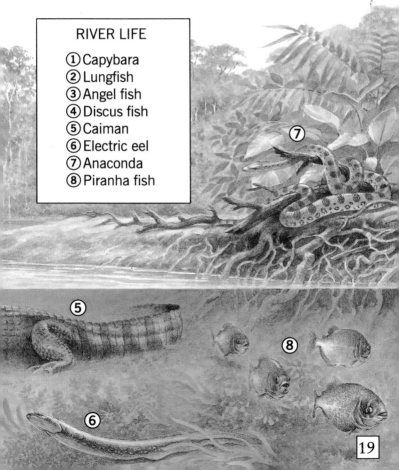

RIVER LIFE

1. Capybara
2. Lungfish
3. Angel fish
4. Discus fish
5. Caiman
6. Electric eel
7. Anaconda
8. Piranha fish

# Insects

The floor of the jungle doesn't get much sunlight, because most of it is blocked out by the leaves overhead. Few plants can grow there, but the ground is covered with rotting leaves and branches. This makes a very good source of food for insects and worms, and for spiders and many other small creatures that feed on insects.

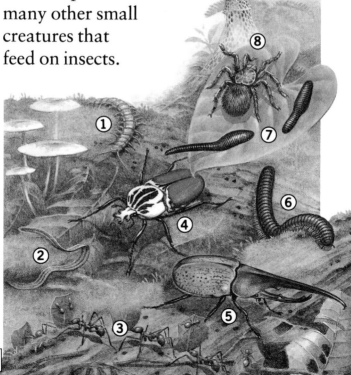

Lots of beautifully colored butterflies and moths fly around in the trees. Most of them feed on the nectar of jungle flowers.

Attract butterflies to your garden with a cotton pad placed in a nectar of honey, sugar, and water.

Morpho cypris

Milionia paradisea

Birdwing

Emperor moth

Heliconius erato

ON THE JUNGLE FLOOR

① Centipede
② Planarian worm
③ Leafcutter ants
④ Goliath beetle
⑤ Hercules beetle
⑥ Millipede
⑦ Leeches
⑧ Bird-eating spider

# Night animals

The jungle is as busy at night as it is during the day. Some night-time animals have big eyes that help them to see in the deep gloom beneath the canopy. Others have a good sense of smell which they use to help them sniff out food.

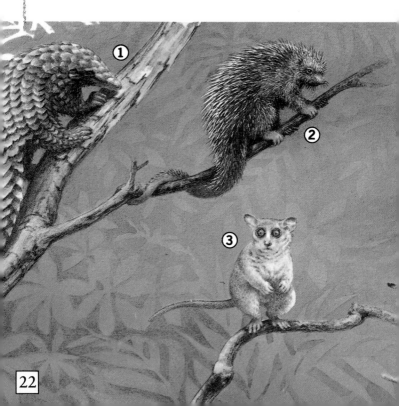

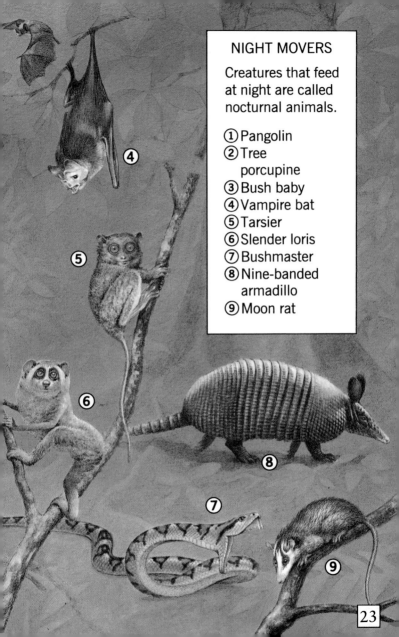

## NIGHT MOVERS

Creatures that feed at night are called nocturnal animals.

① Pangolin
② Tree porcupine
③ Bush baby
④ Vampire bat
⑤ Tarsier
⑥ Slender loris
⑦ Bushmaster
⑧ Nine-banded armadillo
⑨ Moon rat

# In disguise

A lot of jungle animals try to avoid becoming a meal for other animals by using camouflage. This makes them hard to see because they look like part of the jungle scenery. The trouble is, enemies often use the same trick to sneak up without being seen.

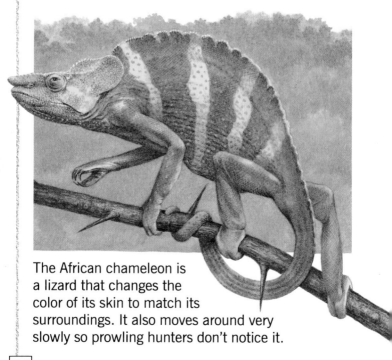

The African chameleon is a lizard that changes the color of its skin to match its surroundings. It also moves around very slowly so prowling hunters don't notice it.

△ Stick insects look like twigs and are almost impossible to spot. A few have flat green bodies that make them look like leaves.

▽ The Gabon viper has a pattern that blends perfectly with the dead leaves on the forest floor.

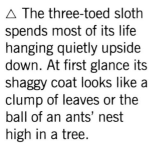

△ The three-toed sloth spends most of its life hanging quietly upside down. At first glance its shaggy coat looks like a clump of leaves or the ball of an ants' nest high in a tree.

# In danger

**M**any of the animals in this book are in danger of dying out. Their main enemies are people who hunt them, or cut down the forests in which they live. In the last 50 years, more kinds of animals have died out, or become extinct, than ever before.

The rhinoceros is one of the most threatened animals in the world. The rarest of all is the Javan rhino of South-east Asia. Laws have now been passed to protect rhinos.

◁ The aye-aye scoops insects out of tree holes with its long, thin, third finger. The aye-aye is nearly extinct and is found only on the island of Madagascar in the Indian Ocean.

▷ The black and white Malayan tapir is a relative of the rhino and the horse. There used to be many tapirs, but now they are found in only a few places.

△ The monkey-eating eagle lives only on the Philippine Islands in the Pacific. About 100 are left and people are trying to save them.

# Kites and masks

J ungle animal shapes and faces are a great way to decorate kites and colorful masks.

You need a large sheet of paper, a length of dowel, a sharp pencil, sticky tape, a spool of thread.

**1** Fold the sheet of paper in half.
**2** Fold back each half to make kite wings.
**3** Turn over and staple the body together. Use the pencil to make a few small holes in the spine of the kite.
**4** Tape over the gap at the front of the kite. Tape down the dowel to stiffen the wings.

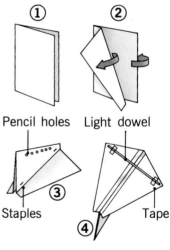

① ②

Pencil holes   Light dowel

③ Staples

④ Tape

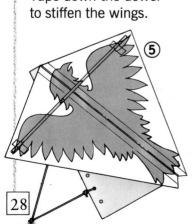

⑤

**5** Thread a length of thread through a hole at one end of the spine and the rest through a hole at the other. Tie the two together. Paint a jungle bird on the front of your kite.

28

# JUNGLE MASKS

You need plain paper plates, elastic, scissors, paint, colored felt-tips, and some wool.

**1** Draw an animal face on a paper plate. Cut out two large holes for the eyes, and two small side holes that will take the elastic.

**2** To hold the mask in place, thread the elastic through the side holes. Tie a knot at the ends.

**3** Add extra bits of decoration to finish off the mask.

Paper plate

Stick on ears made of cardboard

Elastic loop

Paints and felt-tips

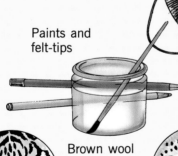

Brown wool fur

# Index